3-Minute

Bible Stories

publications international, ltd.

CONTENTS

Creation

Retold by Brian Conway
Illustrated by Claudine Gévry

In the beginning, there was nothing but God. God created the heavens and the earth. But the earth was empty and dark. God had a plan to give it shape and life.

On the first day, God said, "Let there be light." A brightness filled the earth. God called the light "day." He called the darkness "night."

On the second day, God said, "Let there be space." A big space surrounded the earth. God called the big space "sky."

On the third day, God said, "Let the waters flow and let dry ground appear." The water formed oceans, rivers, lakes, and ponds. The ground formed mountains, valleys, deserts, and islands. God planted trees, grass, and flowers. He gave these plants seeds, so they could bear fruit and grow.

On the fourth day, God looked into the empty sky and said, "Let there be lights in the sky." God created two great lights and hung them in the sky. He called the brighter light "sun." He made the sun shine over the earth during the day. He called the other light "moon." The moon gave the dark night sky a soft glow.

On the fifth day, God looked into the seas. He said, "Let the waters be alive with creatures." To the waters, God added creatures of all sizes, shapes, and colors.

Then God looked again into the big sky. He said, "Let the skies be alive with creatures that fly." God made creatures with wings, which he called "birds." The birds flew playfully across the sky.

God looked upon all that he had created. The land, the plants, the flowing waters, the big sky, the creatures of the seas, the creatures of the skies — they were all good. And God was pleased.

On the sixth day, God said, "Let there be creatures to live upon the land." God created all the animals on the earth. Some were small. Others were tall. Some lived on the ground. Others lived in the ground. Some were loud. Others were quiet. Some moved quickly. Others moved slowly.

In the fields, God placed cows and sheep, horses and buffaloes, rabbits and mice. Soon the woods were filled with squirrels and chipmunks, fast foxes and deers, creeping spiders and insects so small no one but God could see them.

The jungles came alive with fierce tigers, chattering chimpanzees, slithering snakes, and trumpeting elephants. There were animals with long necks and others with stripes and spots. There were animals who came out only at night and animals who would sleep all winter.

God created many animals. Every animal was special in its own way. God wanted all of the creatures to grow and have children.

Then God created another creature on the sixth day. He called this creature "man."

Man was created in God's own image. God made man to watch over all living things.

God blessed this first man. He said, "Live upon this world I have created. Make sure all the world's creatures multiply and prosper." The man received God's blessing.

This is how God created the world from nothing. From darkness, he created light. From emptiness, he created life.

Each thing God created was good, and he was pleased.

Adam and Eve

Retold by Lora Kalkman
Illustrated by Richard Bernal

In the beginning, God created day and night. He created the heavens and the earth. He created all the trees and plants. He created all the birds and all the fish and all the animals. Then he created Adam, the first man.

God wanted Adam to be happy, so he created a glorious garden where Adam could live. It was called the Garden of Eden. God filled the garden with everything Adam could ever want or need. Adam was very pleased with his new home.

The Garden of Eden was the most beautiful place on earth. It was filled with tall trees that provided shade and bright flowers that smelled lovely. It had a clear brook where fish swam.

One day, God brought all the creatures of the earth to the garden so Adam could name them. There were many beautiful and magnificent animals, and Adam happily named each one.

Adam enjoyed his lovely home and all of the animals. Still, God could see that Adam was lonely. God decided to make a partner for Adam. When Adam was asleep, God took one rib from Adam's chest. With it, he created woman. The woman's name was Eve.

Adam loved Eve very much. Eve was Adam's friend and his helper. Adam and Eve were married in the lovely Garden of Eden.

Adam and Eve enjoyed living in the garden. God saw that Adam and Eve were very happy, which pleased him. In exchange for all that he gave them, God expected them to follow just one simple rule.

"You may eat from any tree in the garden, except the Tree of the Knowledge of Good and Evil," God said.

Adam and Eve did not question God. They were grateful to God, and they wanted to obey God's command. Adam and Eve wanted nothing more than to live happily in the garden.

One day, Adam and Eve walked by the Tree of the Knowledge of Good and Evil. Eve noticed the big red apples dangling from its branches. The apples looked delicious, but Eve remembered God's command not to eat from that tree.

Just then, a long black snake slithered along a branch toward Eve. The snake wanted to tempt Eve into disobeying God's rule. "Why don't you eat some apples from this tree?" the snake asked.

"God told us not to eat from this tree," Eve said.

Adam agreed with Eve.

"But if you eat these apples," the snake said, "you will become as smart as God."

Eve wanted to be very smart. She picked two apples from the forbidden tree and gave one to Adam. Eve took a bite of her apple even though she knew she should not. Adam took a bite of his apple even though he knew he should not.

Just then, God went to the garden. He wanted to see Adam and Eve, but he could not find them.

Adam and Eve tried to hide from God. They hid because they were ashamed that they had disobeyed him.

God then realized that they had eaten from the forbidden tree. God was not angry, but he was very sad.

God had no choice but to punish the snake for tricking Adam and Eve. He forced the snake to slither on the ground forever. He made the snake an enemy of men and women.

"The snake will now be able to bite and poison people," God said. "People will now step on the snake."

Then God had to punish Adam and Eve for breaking his rule. He told Adam and Eve they would have to leave the Garden of Eden forever.

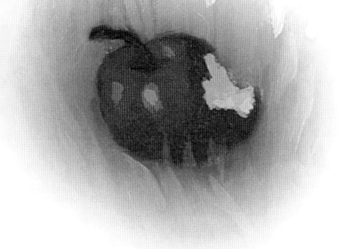

"You will have to plant your own garden and grow your own food," God said. "You will have to work hard to build a new home to protect yourselves from rain and cold."

God gave Adam and Eve clothes. Then he sent them away from the Garden of Eden.

God watched in sorrow as Adam and Eve walked away. He knew that Adam and Eve would be hungry when there was not enough rain to make their garden grow. He knew they would grow tired from cutting and hauling wood to build their house. This made God sad, for even though Adam and Eve had disobeyed him, God still loved them.

Noah's Ark

Retold by Suzanne Lieurance
Illustrated by Carolyn Croll

Once, long ago, the earth had become a very bad place. God was disappointed. He decided the world needed a new beginning.

Noah, his wife, their three sons, and the sons' wives were good people. God knew that Noah and his family would listen to him, so he trusted them with a very serious job.

God told Noah he was going to flood the earth. He told Noah to build a boat for himself and his family. This boat, called an ark, had to be big enough for Noah, all of his family, and a pair of every kind of animal in the world.

Noah started to build the ark. His sons helped him, and his wife and his sons' wives filled the ark with everything they would need to survive.

Noah and his family worked and worked. It took them a long time to build the ark, but finally they finished it. Noah and his family were almost ready for the flood.

The sky slowly darkened, and soon there was a long line of animals parading toward the ark. The animals lined up, two by two, with a male and a female of each kind of animal ready to board the ark. Pairs of zebras and giraffes and elephants lined up. Rabbits, horses, and turtles lined up. Lions, monkeys, and dogs stood in line, too.

Noah helped all the animals climb aboard.

At last, when all the animals had entered, Noah and his family boarded the ark. Noah pulled up the plank and sealed the door shut just as it began to rain.

At first, only tiny drops of water fell, but soon sheets of rain pelted the ark. The ground quickly turned to mud. The mud quickly became big puddles. The puddles quickly became ponds. The ponds quickly became lakes.

It rained and rained. It rained for forty days and for forty nights. Water covered everything in sight. There was no land anywhere. Even the mountains were covered with water. But Noah, his family, and all the animals were safe and dry inside the floating ark. They were all that was left in the world.

Noah and his family felt frightened and lost. They looked out the window, but there was nothing but water. They knew that God would take care of them, though. God had made a promise to Noah.

Finally, the rain stopped. After a while, the water began to sink lower. The ark came to rest on the top of a mountain. Noah and his wife were very happy to reach firm land, but they still did not know if there was dry land to settle on.

Noah decided to release a dove into the air. The dove returned before dark. There was still too much water. Noah waited awhile and then sent the dove out again. This time the dove brought back a branch in its beak.

There was dry land!

Two by two, the animals left the ark. They went in search of homes where they could create new families.

Noah had trusted God. God was so pleased, he decided to make a special promise to Noah. He promised him that he would never bring another great flood.

To mark his promise, God created a beautiful rainbow of colors. He told Noah, "I have put a rainbow in the sky. After each rain, look for it. It is my everlasting promise to you."

Joseph's Coat

Retold by Lisa Harkrader
Illustrated by Stacey Shuett

Joseph held up the coat his father, Jacob, had given him. Joseph's eleven older brothers watched as he put it on. It was made of so many colors it looked like a rainbow. The brothers thought Joseph was their father's favorite son.

That night, Joseph had a strange dream. In this dream, Joseph and his brothers were working in their father's field. They were cutting wheat and tying it into bundles. Joseph's bundle of wheat stood up tall and straight. His brothers' bundles of wheat bowed down low to his bundle of wheat.

"What do you think it means?" Joseph asked his brothers.

"It means you think too much of yourself," said Judah.

"Do you really think we would all bow down to you?" asked Reuben.

That night, Joseph had another dream. In it, the sun, the moon, and eleven stars all bowed down to him. When Joseph woke up, he ran to tell his whole family about his dream.

"What does it mean?" Joseph asked.

This time even Joseph's father was shocked by the dream. But Jacob did not forget about it. He wondered if the dream would ever come true.

One day, when Joseph's older brothers were tending their father's flocks in the field, Jacob sent Joseph to help them. When Joseph reached his brothers they grabbed him, tore off his many-colored coat, and threw him into an empty well. Later, they sold him to a trade caravan. They did all this because they were jealous of the way their father loved Joseph.

Then the brothers tore the many-colored coat to shreds. They dipped it in goat's blood and gave it to their father.

"No!" Jacob cried. "My son Joseph is dead!"

But Joseph was not dead. The traders sold Joseph to Pharaoh's officials. Pharaoh was the ruler of Egypt. The officials put Joseph in charge of Pharaoh's jail. The prisoners trusted Joseph and began to tell him their dreams.

Joseph explained the dreams, and everything he told them came true. Then Pharaoh began to have strange dreams. The officials brought Joseph to Pharaoh. Pharaoh told Joseph his dreams.

"In one dream," said Pharaoh, "seven fat cows ate thick grass. Then seven skinny cows came and swallowed the fat cows. In another dream, seven plump ears of corn sprouted on a cornstalk. Then seven withered ears of corn sprouted and swallowed the good corn. What does it all mean?"

"For the next seven years, Egypt will have more food than the people can eat," said Joseph. "Then the rain will stop. For seven years after that, Egypt will not be able to grow enough food to feed the people."

Joseph told Pharaoh to store extra grain during the seven good years. During the seven bad years, the people would have enough to eat.

Pharaoh appointed Joseph to oversee the harvests. Joseph became the highest official in all of Egypt. The only person more powerful than Joseph was Pharaoh.

For seven years, the land of Egypt had good crops, and Joseph stored grain. At the end of those seven years, all the crops died, but Joseph had stored enough food.

In the land of Canaan, where Joseph's family lived, the people had not stored grain. They were hungry. Jacob heard about the grain in Egypt. He gathered his ten oldest sons and gave them sacks of silver.

Jacob sent his sons to Egypt to buy grain. The brothers were brought before Joseph. Joseph recognized them at once.

But Joseph decided not to tell them who he was. "Are you your father's only sons?" Joseph asked.

"There are two more," Reuben said. "Joseph is gone. Benjamin stayed home."

"I'll sell you the grain you need, but you must bring Benjamin back to me," said Joseph. "I'll keep your brother Simeon here in Egypt until you return."

Joseph told his assistant to fill his brothers' sacks with grain. Then he ordered them to secretly put his brothers' silver back into the sacks before tying them shut.

When Joseph's brothers returned to Canaan, they were surprised to find the silver in their sacks. Their father was furious that they had left Simeon behind.

"But if we take Benjamin to meet Pharaoh's high official," Reuben explained, "he'll let Simeon go."

"I won't risk Benjamin's life," Jacob said. "Pharaoh's official must think you stole that silver from him."

Soon, though, Jacob's family needed more food. Jacob had to send his sons to Egypt again.

The brothers went to Egypt, and they took Benjamin with them. Joseph was happy to see his brothers again. Joseph told his assistant to fill their bags with grain and to secretly place his favorite cup in Benjamin's bag.

Joseph's brothers had not gone far when Joseph's assistant stopped them. He searched the bags and found Joseph's cup in Benjamin's sack of grain.

"You are free to go," Joseph said, "but Benjamin stays here."

"We are brothers," said Reuben. "If Benjamin stays, we all stay."

Joseph was happy to hear that his brothers would not abandon Benjamin. "I'm your brother, too," he said. "It is me Joseph."

Joseph's brothers could not believe their eyes. Joseph sent for his father and for his brothers' families. Pharaoh gave them all land to live on.

"There was a reason my brothers sold me," said Joseph. "God wanted me in Egypt. He wanted me to save Egypt and my family."

Ruth and Naomi

Retold by Leslie Lindecker
Illustrated by Holly Jones

Naomi lived for many years in a country called Moab. She had traveled there with her husband and two sons. They made a happy life together.

Her sons grew up and married two young women from Moab. Their names were Orpah and Ruth.

Then Naomi's husband became ill, and he passed away. Naomi's sons also got sick and died. This left Naomi, Orpah, and Ruth alone and very sad.

Without her husband, Naomi decided to return to her home in Bethlehem.

"The two of you should return to your families here in Moab," Naomi said to Orpah and Ruth. "You are both young enough to marry again and have children."

"I will miss you," Orpah said. "You've been so kind to me."

The thought of leaving Naomi made Ruth very sad. "I will not leave you," Ruth said. "Where you go, I will go."

Naomi was happy Ruth wanted to stay with her. They began their walk to Bethlehem. They arrived there just as the grain harvest began.

Ruth turned to Naomi and said, "Let me go into the fields. I can gather the grain dropped by the workers and bake bread for us to eat."

Naomi rested. Ruth walked behind the workers, gathering the grain they dropped as they worked. She worked all day.

Late in the afternoon, a man named Boaz came to the field. He was in charge of the workers.

He noticed Ruth and asked one of the workers about her.

"She is Ruth from Moab," the worker said. "She traveled here with Naomi and asked to gather the dropped grain so they would have something to eat. Since she is such a great help to Naomi, we did not think you would mind."

Boaz did not mind. In fact, he was pleased to help Ruth and Naomi. He introduced himself to Ruth.

"I have heard good things about you," said Boaz. "You take care of your mother-in-law. You are kind to others and help my workers. Please continue to work in my fields. When you are thirsty, please drink from my water pots. When I bring food for my workers, I want you to eat with them."

"May God bless you," Ruth said.

When Boaz brought food for his workers, Ruth ate with them. She saved part of her food and took it to Naomi.

Naomi was pleased with the food and grain. "Who was this man who gave you food and grain?" Naomi asked.

"His name is Boaz," Ruth said. "He said that I may continue to work in the fields."

"Boaz is the brother of my husband," Naomi said. "He is a good and kind man."

"May God bless him for his kindness and generosity toward us," Ruth said.

Boaz continued to watch Ruth as she worked in his fields. He talked with her often and also saw how much she loved Naomi. Boaz became very fond of Ruth, and Ruth became very fond of Boaz.

Boaz went to Ruth one day and said, "I would like for you to be my wife. Your mother-in-law, Naomi, may live with us. I would like to take care of you both."

Ruth and Boaz were soon married. Naomi lived with them in their new home, and she was very happy.

Then Ruth had a baby boy. She named the baby Obed, and they all thanked God for the blessings of home and of family.

Samuel

Retold by Lisa Harkrader
Illustrated by Jon Goodell

Elkanah married Peninnah and Hannah. Long ago, men could marry more than one woman. Peninnah had many children, but Hannah had not been able to have even one child. Still, Elkanah loved her very much.

One day, Elkanah saw Hannah playing with Peninnah's children. Hannah smiled, but she was sad.

Elkanah gave Hannah a beautiful scarf stitched with gold thread. "I hope this will cheer you up," he said.

"Thank you," Hannah said.

Peninnah saw the gift Elkanah had given Hannah. She waited until Elkanah left, then she said, "It upsets Elkanah that you haven't had any children."

Hannah believed this was true.

"He only gives you gifts because he feels sorry for you," Peninnah said.

Peninnah had more children. Hannah did not. She did not understand why God had not given her a child, too.

Finally, Hannah traveled to Shiloh to pray in God's temple. "Please, God," she whispered. "If you could see fit to give me a son, I promise he will spend his life serving you."

Hannah prayed for so long that the priest of the temple, Eli, noticed her.

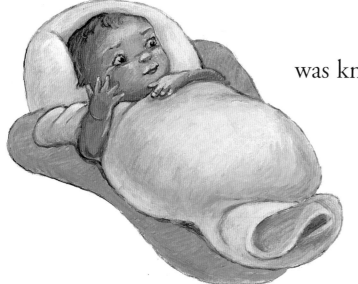

Eli came over to where Hannah was kneeling and asked her if she was ill. "I am not ill," Hannah said, "but something is wrong. God has not blessed me with a child. I'm praying for a baby. I want to give my husband a son."

Eli blessed Hannah and told her to go in peace. She went home, and soon she discovered she was going to have a baby!

"I want to name him Samuel," Hannah said when the baby was born. "It means, 'asked of the Lord.' Our son was born because I prayed to God."

"Then Samuel will be his name," said Elkanah.

Samuel grew to be a strong and healthy boy. His mother loved him and took good care of him, but she never forgot the promise she had made to God.

When Samuel was old enough, Hannah and Elkanah took him to the temple in Shiloh. It was the same temple where Hannah had prayed for a child. There they found Eli.

"God has given us a son," Hannah told Eli. "I must keep my promise to God."

Hannah kissed Samuel and held him tight. "You must live in the temple with Eli now," she said. "He will take care of you and teach you to serve God."

Samuel learned from Eli as much as he could about serving God and being a priest.

Samuel grew up to be an honest and hardworking man. Eli had two sons who lived in the temple, too. These sons were not honest like Samuel. They were greedy and sneaky.

One night, after Samuel had gone to bed, he heard someone call his name. He thought it must be Eli, so he went to him. "Why did you call me?" Samuel asked.

Eli woke up. "I didn't call you, Samuel," he said. "God must be calling you. Go back to your bed and say, 'Speak, Lord. I am your servant, and I am listening.'"

Samuel went back to bed. "Speak, Lord," he said. "I am your servant, and I am listening."

God said, "Eli's sons have brought shame to the temple."

The next morning, Samuel told Eli what God had said.

"It is true," Eli said. "My sons do not honor God. You, Samuel, will become the temple priest."

Samuel

When Eli died, Samuel took Eli's place at the temple. Samuel had sons of his own by this time, but just like Eli's sons, they had become sneaky and greedy. The people of Israel knew Samuel's sons would take his place at the temple someday, and they did not want to be ruled by greedy men who did not honor God.

"Other nations are ruled by a king," they said.

"God is Israel's king," Samuel said.

"God will not speak to us through priests who bring shame to the temple," the people said. "We need a king."

Samuel prayed to God.

"Tomorrow I will send to you Saul from the land of Benjamin," God said. "He will become the first king of Israel."

David and Goliath

Retold by Catherine McCafferty
Illustrated by Anthony Lewis

David was a good shepherd and a good harp player, but when God sent the prophet Samuel to name David as the next king of Israel, David was surprised.

He was ready to go to the palace right away, but Samuel told him to continue tending the sheep for his father because David's brothers had to join the army. Saul, who was Israel's present king, needed help fighting the Philistines. David wished he could go with his brothers to prove himself.

One morning, as David watched the sheep, a lion ran off with a lamb. David chased the lion. He aimed a stone at the lion with his sling and hit the beast in the head! The lion dropped the lamb and ran away.

"I hope to be a brave soldier and a good king," David said.

David's chance to prove himself came, but not as he expected. King Saul was worried about the war and needed some music to soothe him. The king heard that David was a good harp player, and David's father agreed to let his son play for the king in the evening. David played for the king every night until the king fell asleep. The king grew fond of David.

When David's brothers had been at war for forty days, their father sent David to the battlefront with food. When David got there, the soldiers were shouting. David left the food with a guard and hurried to the soldiers.

Goliath, the Philistines' leader, had stepped onto the battlefield. He was a giant! His armor alone looked as if it weighed more than David. The spear Goliath carried looked mighty enough to stab the sky.

"Choose one man to fight against me," roared Goliath. "If he kills me, the Philistines will be your slaves. If I kill him, you shall become our slaves."

Most of the soldiers ran away, and David realized this was his chance to prove himself. He went to the king and said, "I will fight Goliath."

"You cannot fight him," Saul said. "You are only a boy."

David described his battle with the lion. "I will defeat Goliath just as I did the lion," he said. "God will protect me."

The king ordered his servant to bring a suit of armor, and David tried it on. It was so heavy David could not move. Saul gave David a large sword, but David could not lift it.

David took off the armor. Then he gathered five stones. He pulled out his sling. He was ready to face Goliath.

Goliath looked down at David and laughed.

David said, "You come against me with a mighty spear, but I come against you in the name of God."

As Goliath's shadow fell over him, David loaded the sling and whirled the stone. Goliath raised his spear. David took aim and let the stone fly.

As the stone hit his forehead, Goliath dropped his spear and crashed to the ground. David had beaten Goliath!

Saul said to David, "From this day forward, you shall be the commander of my army!"

David bowed to Saul, accepting his new position. Then he took Goliath's armor and spear. David wanted them as reminders of God's power. With God beside him, David did not have to be big to be brave.

Elijah and Elisha

Retold by Elizabeth Olson
Illustrated by Lyn Martin

King Ahab was a bad king who worshiped false gods. Elijah the prophet did God's work and served the Lord well. One day, God punished Ahab by sending a drought to Ahab's kingdom.

Elijah delivered the news to the king. "King Ahab," said Elijah, because you do not listen to the word of God, no rain will fall in your kingdom for many years."

God loved Elijah and wanted to protect him. "Elijah, you must leave the kingdom of Ahab," said God. "I will show you a safe place to live."

God led Elijah to a lovely brook in the hills. "Here you will be safe," said God. "You can drink from this clear stream. Every day, a raven will bring you bread and meat to eat."

For several years, Elijah lived in the beautiful place in the hills. The friendly raven made sure that Elijah always had enough to eat. Elijah gave thanks to God for his blessings.

One day the stream stopped running, and the raven did not appear. God said, "Elijah, you are a faithful servant. Now you must go to Sidon. A kind woman there will take care of you."

Elijah obeyed God.

At the city gate of Sidon, he met the woman. "I am very hungry," he said. "Could you please give me a small piece of bread?"

"I would gladly give you what I have," she said, "but I have barely enough flour and oil to make bread for my son."

"God will not let you go hungry," said Elijah. "Make a small loaf of bread for me from what you have. Then make a loaf for your son and another for yourself. Your oil and flour will never run out."

Elijah the prophet continued to serve God for many years. One day, God sent him to Damascus.

"You are getting older, Elijah," said God. "The time has come for you to have a helper. Go and find Elisha."

Elijah obeyed God. He soon found Elisha plowing a field. Elijah put his coat over the young man's shoulders. Elisha understood the will of God. Together the two men walked through the fields.

When the two men came upon the River Jordan, Elijah touched the blessed coat to the river. Elisha could not believe his eyes as the water divided to create a dry path.

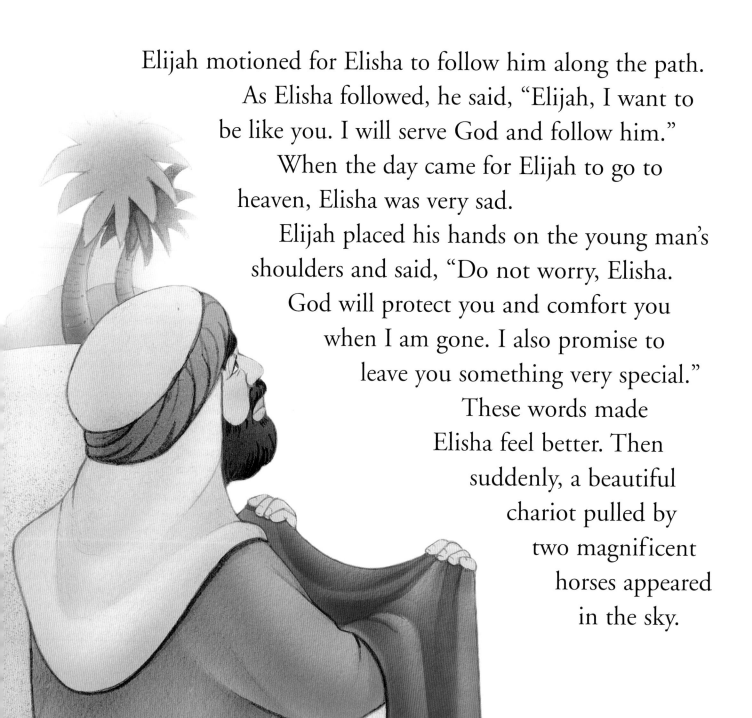

Elijah motioned for Elisha to follow him along the path. As Elisha followed, he said, "Elijah, I want to be like you. I will serve God and follow him."

When the day came for Elijah to go to heaven, Elisha was very sad.

Elijah placed his hands on the young man's shoulders and said, "Do not worry, Elisha. God will protect you and comfort you when I am gone. I also promise to leave you something very special."

These words made Elisha feel better. Then suddenly, a beautiful chariot pulled by two magnificent horses appeared in the sky.

The horses
came down from the sky
and stopped right in front of Elijah.
"I must go to heaven now," said Elijah.
"Goodbye, Elisha, my friend."
Elijah climbed into the chariot, which immediately began
to rise back into the clouds.

"I will miss you!" called Elisha.

Just then, Elisha noticed that Elijah had dropped his wonderful coat on the ground. This must be the special gift that Elijah promised to leave him.

Elisha picked up the coat. It would always make him think of Elijah. He also knew that, through the coat, God was comforting and protecting him.

Elisha missed his friend, but he continued to serve God and help others. He often gave all he had to people who needed it, and other people helped him.

One woman offered him bread. She offered him bread whenever he walked past her house.

"You have been very kind to me," Elisha said to her one day. "There must be something I can do for you in return."

"My husband and I would like to have a child," she said. "We have everything we need and could take good care of a child, but I do not think you can help me with that."

"I will pray to God," Elisha said. "You have been kind to me and God will take care of you."

Elisha prayed to God to bring the couple a child. God answered his prayers. The woman soon had a baby, and she and her husband were very happy.

Elisha was happy, too.

Esther

Retold by Kate Hannigan
Illustrated by Sally Schaedler

I n the days of King Ahasuerus, there lived a young woman named Esther. Esther had lost her parents, so her uncle, Mordecai, raised her as his own.

Esther was smart and beautiful, and she had a good heart. She was kind to everyone she met, from the bakers to the shepherds to the servants of the king. When the king met Esther, he fell deeply in love with her.

"I will hold a feast for Esther," said the king.

At the feast, the king declared Esther his queen.

The king and Esther were married. Uncle Mordecai was very happy for Esther.

But at her wedding, he overheard two men talking in secret. These men wanted to do harm to the king.

"The king must be warned," Mordecai thought.

Mordecai ran to tell Esther what he heard. In turn, Esther told the king. The king severely punished the men.

"Mordecai," said the king, "you saved my life."

The king had many advisers to help him govern his large kingdom. His top adviser was a man named Haman, who loved power. "People should bow down before me!" Haman thought.

Many people did bow before Haman, but Mordecai, who was Jewish, refused to bow to false idols. This made Haman angry, and he plotted to hurt Mordecai. "Mordecai and his people will be punished," Haman said.

Haman went to the king with a plan. He said there were certain people in the kingdom who would not follow the laws.

"We must destroy them," Haman urged.

The king agreed. He gave Haman his ring, which bore the official seal of the kingdom, and every province was told about the plan to attack the Jews on a specific day Haman had chosen.

Mordecai heard about Haman's plan and told Esther. "The king must help our people," Mordecai said.

Esther was Jewish. She had never told the king. Now her life was in danger. All the Jews were going to be destroyed.

"I will ask him to help us," Esther said.

It was dangerous to ask the king for favors. If he did not like what he heard, the king could deliver a harsh punishment.

Still, people traveled from all corners of the kingdom to speak with him. Esther paced nervously among the crowd in the courtyard, knowing it would be hard to ask anything of the king. She was risking her life. But when the king saw her standing among the rest of the people, he called to her.

"What is it, my beloved Esther?" he asked.

Esther was afraid, but she had a plan. Her hands trembled as she knelt before the king.

"I am hosting a banquet tonight," she said. "I would like you and your adviser Haman to attend."

The king and Haman went to Esther's party. They ate good food and listened to fine music.

"What do you want, dear Esther?" asked the king.

"I enjoy your company so much," Esther said, "I would like you to come again tomorrow night. I will tell you then."

The king was happy. Haman was also happy. They liked parties, and Esther was good company. They said they would come again the next night.

The day after Esther's first party, the king met with his advisers to discuss the business of his large and vast kingdom.

The king wanted to know how Mordecai had been rewarded for saving his life. His advisers told him Mordecai had not been rewarded.

"Call in my chief adviser!" shouted the king, and Haman was summoned to the king's office. "What shall we do to reward the man who saved my life?"

In his arrogance, Haman thought the king wanted to reward him. "He should be dressed in the finest robes and led through town on a beautiful horse," said Haman.

"Good plan," said the king. "Now hurry with the finest robes and a beautiful horse to carry Mordecai through the town. Tell everyone how he saved the king's life!"

Haman was furious. "This is an insult!" he thought. "I must get rid of Mordecai as soon as possible!"

That night, Esther had another banquet.

"What is your wish, dear Esther?" asked the king.

"Someone wants to hurt my people," Esther said.

"Who is trying to hurt your people?" asked the king.

"That wicked man!" said Esther, pointing at Haman. "I am Jewish, and Haman wants to hurt all the Jewish people."

The king banished Haman. He gave Mordecai Haman's job. Soon Mordecai found out that a specific day had been chosen by Haman to attack the Jews.

"Haman has sent soldiers to hurt my people," Esther told the king. "Let me warn my people so they can defend themselves."

The king gave Esther his ring with the royal seal, but Esther and Mordecai still had to act fast. They sent riders to every province, telling the Jewish people to rise up and defend themselves. The king's messengers rode as fast as they could to deliver the news. They were able to warn the Jews just in time.

Esther's people waged a fierce battle and defeated Haman's soldiers. Instead of a day of massacre, it was a day of great triumph for the Jews.

Daniel in the Lions' Den

Retold by Virginia R. Biles
Illustrated by Cathy Jones

When Daniel was a boy, Judah was conquered by King Nebuchadnezzar. Daniel's people, who were the Jews, were taken as prisoners.

Daniel was a prisoner, but he was taken to the king's palace to live. All the smart boys went to live at the palace. The king planned to teach them all about their new country and to make them great leaders. Daniel and his friends were happy there, but Daniel continued to worship God.

God was pleased with Daniel as he grew into a young man. God rewarded him by giving him a special gift. Daniel could interpret dreams.

One night the king had a dream. He called his wise men and asked them to interpret the dream.

None of them could explain the dream to the king.

When Daniel heard this he said, "I will go to the king. God has given me a gift. I can interpret dreams and visions."

Daniel told the king what the dream meant. The king was so pleased that he placed Daniel in a high position and gave him many gifts.

Later the king sent for Daniel again. He told Daniel about another dream.

Daniel said, "It means you will live with the wild animals for seven years, until you follow God."

"I will never live with the wild animals," said King Nebuchadnezzar. "I am a great king!"

God was not happy with this king who was so full of pride. No sooner were the words out of his mouth than he became like an animal. He tore his clothes. He ran away to the woods and lived with the wild animals. His hair grew long, and his nails were like the claws of a bird.

At the end of seven long years, King Nebuchadnezzar saw the error of his ways and praised God. Then God returned his mind to him. Nebuchadnezzar spent the rest of his days praising God.

When King Nebuchadnezzar died, his son Belshazzar became the king. One night during a banquet, the king and his guests saw a ghostly finger writing on the wall of the dining room. The king's face grew very pale, and his knees grew very weak.

King Belshazzar called for his advisers. "What does this mean?" he asked them.

When they could not tell him, he grew even paler and more frightened. Then someone remembered Daniel. The king sent for Daniel.

"What does this mean?" King Belshazzar asked. "If you can tell me, I will make you the third highest ruler in the kingdom and give you riches."

"It means that your kingdom will be taken by your enemies," Daniel said.

And that very night, King Belshazzar was killed in battle and his kingdom was taken by King Darius.

King Darius had heard of wise Daniel, and he made him one of his top three rulers. He even planned to make Daniel his top adviser.

The other wise men were jealous of Daniel. They wanted to get rid of him. They went to King Darius and said, "You should make a law that declares that anyone who prays to any god or man, instead of you, will be thrown into the lions' den."

King Darius made it a law. After Daniel heard about the new law he prayed to God, just as he did before.

The wise men spied on Daniel. They listened at his door and heard him praying to God. They now had something to use against Daniel, and they presented it to King Darius.

"You made a law. Anyone who prays to any god or man, instead of you, will be thrown into the lions' den," the wise men said. "Daniel has broken that law."

"Bring Daniel to me," the king said. King Darius knew that he had been tricked by his wise men. He did not want to kill Daniel, but he had made the law.

King Darius put his hand on Daniel's shoulder and said, "May your God rescue you from the lions."

Soldiers led Daniel from the palace to a cave with a deep pit. The pit held hungry lions. They put Daniel in the pit with the lions. Then they rolled a large rock in front of the the cave, so no one could rescue Daniel.

At dawn the next day, King Darius called the soldiers and hurried on foot to the lions' den. "Daniel!" shouted the king. "Has your God rescued you from the lions? Are you alive?"

"Yes, I am alive," Daniel said. "God shut the lions' mouths because I am innocent in God's sight. I have not wronged you."

The soldiers rolled the rock away from the cave, and Daniel was lifted from the den. He was unharmed.

King Darius punished the men who had accused Daniel. He had them put in the lions' den, but God did not shut the lions' mouths because these men were not innocent.

Then King Darius made Daniel his most trusted adviser. Over the rest of his life, Daniel interpreted many dreams and visions for the king.

Jonah and the Whale

Retold by Brian Conway
Illustrated by Laura Merer

Jonah was one of God's faithful servants. He lived a simple life in a quiet village. He prayed to God and followed all of God's commandments.

One day, God chose Jonah for a very special task. God wanted Jonah to take a journey to a nearby city. The city, called Nineveh, had turned to sin and violence.

"The people in Nineveh have forgotten me," God said. "Go to that city, Jonah, and bring the people my word."

Jonah had heard many frightful stories about the city of Nineveh. It was a terrible place. People were sinful there. They were often mean to each other, and they were always mean to strangers.

Jonah was afraid. He did not want to go to Nineveh.

In his fear, Jonah thought only of saving himself. He did not think of God's wishes. He ran away from God, instead.

Jonah thought he could hide from God in a faraway place. In a seaport, he found a boat that was about to leave for a distant land. He paid his fare and climbed aboard the boat.

The ship sailed, and Jonah went below the deck. There, he fell asleep. He slept until a great storm rose from the sea.

"What is happening?" Jonah asked a passenger.

"A terrible storm came upon us suddenly," the passenger replied. "We are in serious danger."

The passengers huddled together inside the boat. They prayed to many different gods to save them. Jonah saw the fear in their faces, but he did not pray. He knew that God had sent the storm, and he knew he was a fool to think he could hide from God.

Jonah said, "The storm is meant for me. I ran away from God. Throw me into the waves, and you will be saved."

The men did as Jonah asked. As soon as he disappeared beneath the waves, the storm stopped.

A giant whale came up from the depths of the sea. It swallowed Jonah in one swift gulp. Like the terrible storm, this giant whale was sent by God. Jonah understood that.

Jonah sat inside the belly of the whale and waited. It was very dark and damp, but at least he was able to breathe again.

Jonah thought for a long time about what had happened. "I should have done as God asked," he whispered.

Jonah was happy to be alive, but he was trapped inside the whale. He wondered if he would ever be free again. Jonah knew that he was not completely alone. God, he understood, was always with him. Jonah asked God to forgive him.

"I was afraid," Jonah prayed, "and I ran away from you. I should have known that you would keep me safe. I know you will keep me safe, God. I trust you more than ever."

Jonah spent three days and three nights inside the whale.

Jonah and the Whale

He was not afraid. He had faith in God's goodness. In his prayers, Jonah promised to always serve God.

Finally, the whale opened its mouth and Jonah was free. He swam to the shore.

God said, "Go to Nineveh as I ask, and bring the people my message."

This time Jonah obeyed. He went to Nineveh.

He warned the people of Nineveh that they could not run away from God. The people listened to his story. And Jonah spread God's message to the people, and they were saved.

The Birth of Jesus

Retold by Suzanne Lieurance
Illustrated by Debbie Pinkney

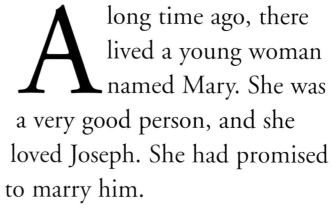

A long time ago, there lived a young woman named Mary. She was a very good person, and she loved Joseph. She had promised to marry him.

One day, God sent the angel Gabriel to visit Mary.

"Do not be afraid, Mary," said Gabriel. "I have wonderful news for you. You have found favor with God. You will be with child and give birth to a son. You shall name the child Jesus."

"How could this be?" Mary asked. "I am not yet married."

"The Holy Spirit will visit you," Gabriel said. "The holy one to be born will be called the Son of God."

"I am the Lord's servant," Mary said.

The angel smiled and floated away.

Months passed. Mary was nearly ready to deliver her baby, but first she and Joseph had to go to Bethlehem to pay taxes. Mary rode a donkey. It was a very long ride, but Mary did not complain.

As the sky grew dark, Joseph looked for a place to spend the night. He knocked on the doors of many inns, but all the rooms were taken. At the last inn Joseph could find, the innkeeper shook his head, too.

"I am sorry," the innkeeper said, "we have no room."

"Please," Joseph said. "Mary is about to deliver her baby."

"I suppose you can stay in the stable with the animals," the innkeeper said. "It is warm there."

Joseph took Mary and the donkey to the stable. He tried to make Mary as comfortable as he could. He cleared a space for her and made a bed out of soft hay so she could rest.

That night, Mary gave birth to her baby. Just as the angel Gabriel told her to do, she named him Jesus.

Mary and Joseph gazed with joy at the tiny baby.

Mary carefully wrapped the baby in strips of soft cloth to keep him warm. They did not have a cradle for the baby, so Joseph laid him to sleep in the manger. The baby fell asleep instantly.

While Jesus, Mary, and Joseph were sleeping, other wonderful things were happening. In a nearby field, some shepherd boys were tending their sheep. Suddenly, a brilliant light filled the sky.

"Look!" one of the boys said.

The other boy looked up to see that a beautiful, bright shining star had appeared in the night sky.

As the shepherd boys gazed at
the star, the sky filled with angels.
The angels looked down
at the shepherd boys
and smiled. Then one
of the angels spoke.

"Do not be frightened," said the angel, "for we come with great news for you. The world shall rejoice! On this day, in the city of Bethlehem, a savior has been born to you. He is Christ the Lord. Go and see him. Witness the miracle. You will find a baby wrapped in cloths and lying in a manger. Follow the shining star. It will lead you to Bethlehem."

Then, as suddenly as they had come, the angels were gone.

The shepherds looked at one another with amazement. "Come," said one of the boys. "We must go."

In Bethlehem, the star was shining directly over the tiny stable. The shepherd boys quietly opened the door to the stable and went in. There they found Mary and Joseph and the baby. Just as the angel had said, the baby was lying in a manger. The shepherds knelt down before the baby to pray.

As the boys prayed, other shepherds gathered behind them. They had all followed the star. They had all come from far away to meet the little baby Jesus. They had all come to witness the beautiful miracle.

John the Baptist

Retold by Michelle Conway
Illustrated by Renée Daily

John the Baptist wandered through the forest each day. He ate berries and locusts. At night, he slept under a canopy of tree branches. He was very happy living in the wilderness.

John was living in the wilderness to be closer to God. He wanted to follow God and obey his rules.

Even though John lived in the wilderness, he still spoke to many people in Judea about God. "The kingdom of God is at hand," John told the people. "The Messiah will soon appear to us."

John brought God's message to the people. He wanted them to be sorry for all of their sins. God wanted John to baptize the people. John listened carefully and obeyed God.

John began preaching in the country surrounding the Jordan River. "You must confess your sins," John told the people. "Come to the river to be baptized."

The people listened. They followed John to the river.

John wore a cloak made from camel's hair. He even ate wild honey. He was very different, but people listened to him.

People from all over were coming to the River Jordan to be baptized by John.

When the first group of people arrived at the river, John asked them, "Why have you come?"

"We have come to confess all of our sins," the people said.

John told the people by the river how to live better lives. He told them to follow all of God's laws.

One man came forward to be baptized. "I am ready to confess," he said.

John led the man into the river. He gathered some water in his hands and poured it over the man's head. He said, "I baptize you in the name of God the Father."

The people in the crowd thought John was very wise. They began to wonder if he was the Messiah. "Could you be the one we have been waiting for?" they asked.

John said, "I baptize you with water, but someone will come who is much more powerful than I. He will baptize you with the Holy Spirit."

John continued to baptize the people until he heard some of them whispering. The crowd parted, and a man walked toward the river.

The mysterious man waded into the river up to his knees. He stopped in front of John the Baptist. "I have come to be baptized by you," he said.

John fell to his knees and bowed his head. The stranger put his hand on John's shoulder.

"It must be Jesus," the people said.

"Will you baptize me, John?" Jesus asked.

"I am not worthy to baptize you," John said.

"God has chosen you," said Jesus.

"You should be the one baptizing me," John said, "but I would be honored to baptize you as God wants."

John gathered water in his hand and poured it over Jesus' head. "In the name of God the Father, I baptize you," he said.

Jesus bowed his head to be baptized.

Just then, the clouds opened up. The sun shone down on Jesus.

A white dove flew from the sky and hovered above Jesus' head.

Jesus smiled and said to all the people, "This is the Holy Spirit. God has sent this beautiful bird because he is pleased. He loves all of you just as he loves me."

After Jesus was baptized, more people came forward. They wanted John to baptize them, too.

And after that, it was time for Jesus to begin traveling and teaching people about God.

The Twelve Disciples

Retold by Leslie Lindecker
Illustrated by Kallen Godsey

A girl named Sarah lived with her family near the Sea of Galilee. One day, Sarah's parents took her to the seashore to hear a teacher, named Jesus, speak. When they got to the Sea of Galilee, many people were gathered there. The fishermen were cleaning their nets on the shore. Jesus climbed into one of the fishing boats. "Simon Peter," Jesus said to one of the fishermen, "please take me out onto the water so everyone can hear me."

As Simon Peter rowed the boat out a short distance, everyone on the shore sat down to listen to Jesus speak. Sarah sat in her father's lap.

Jesus talked for a long time. He told stories Sarah could understand. Everyone around Sarah and her family kept very quiet so they could hear everything Jesus said.

After Jesus had finished speaking, he turned to Simon Peter and said, "Cast your nets and catch fish to feed all these hungry people."

"Teacher," said Simon Peter, "we fished all night. We did not catch any fish, but we will try again."

Simon Peter returned Jesus to the shore and then went back out to sea to cast his nets. At once the nets were full of fish! The nets were so heavy with fish, Simon Peter was afraid they might break.

Simon Peter waved at his partners James and John. James and John rowed a second boat out and helped Simon Peter pull the nets up into the two boats.

Simon Peter, James, and John rowed the boats back to the shore. Sarah's father and the other men on the shore helped them unload all the fish. Everyone had plenty to eat.

After the meal, Jesus spoke to Simon Peter, James, and John. "You have been good fishermen," he said. "Now I want you to come with me and be fishers of men, helping me teach everyone about God."

Later that week, Sarah's father came home. He was very excited. He told the family that Jesus had come to the village where Sarah and her family lived. Jesus met with the priests at the temple.

Outside the temple, a tax collector named Matthew was taking taxes from the people coming out of the temple. Jesus went up to Matthew and said, "Follow me."

Matthew walked with Jesus from the tax booth and left behind the money he had collected. Together, they went to Matthew's home and ate dinner.

The priests were very unhappy. They grumbled about Jesus choosing a tax collector to follow him. They said Matthew was the worst kind of sinner, and they were surprised that Jesus would sit down to eat with such a man.

Jesus said to them, "I call all people to follow me. Remember, God loves everyone, including the sinners and the tax collectors. They are the lost sheep who need God's love most of all."

Sarah's family learned that Jesus was traveling to each of the towns and villages in the area. He spoke in the temples from dawn to dusk.

Then the people from these villages would come to Jesus. They wanted to be healed by him, and they wanted to hear his wonderful stories.

Sarah's mother said, "Jesus tells us that we are like sheep without a shepherd. He says that he is the shepherd sent by God to gather the flock of sheep close to God."

"Jesus has chosen twelve men to learn from him and to help him teach," said Sarah's father.

"Yes," said Sarah's mother. "The men will learn the ways of God and teach others about them. It is an important thing."

"Jesus chose Simon Peter, James, and John, the fishermen we saw at the seashore," said Sarah's father. "He also chose Matthew the tax collector and men named Bartholomew, Philip, Judas, and Andrew. There are men named Thomas, James, and Simon. The last man is named Judas Iscariot."

These men traveled with Jesus wherever he went. They were his disciples. They learned from him and helped him teach everyone about the love of God.

Jesus invited all of his followers to join him and his disciples. Sarah and her family sat and listened quietly as Jesus spoke to his disciples.

"You will have the power to heal the sick, cleanse the spirit, and chase away demons," Jesus said to them. "Seek the lost sheep of God's world and lead them back to his love. As you go, tell them, 'The kingdom of heaven is at hand,' and they will know you have been sent by the Son of God."

Jesus instructed his disciples. Together they were able to teach everyone about the love of God.

The First Miracle

Retold by Elizabeth Olson
Illustrated by Lynda Calvert-Weyant

Jesus, his disciples, and his mother, Mary, attended a grand wedding in Galilee. The guests danced, laughed, and ate. When they were thirsty, servants brought them goblets of wine from big stone jugs.

Mary was one of the happiest guests. She was happy to be near her son. She loved to watch him speak with his new disciples. They were talking about God's love.

When Jesus had finished speaking with his disciples, the disciples left Jesus alone with his mother.

"Jesus," Mary said, "I am so proud of you for spreading the word of God. You are a blessing to his name."

"Thank you very much," said Jesus. "I hope also to be a blessing to you."

The musicians started to play a joyful song. All the guests jumped up to dance.

"Mother, would you care to dance with me?" Jesus asked.

"Oh, yes," said Mary, beaming.

Jesus and Mary joined the other guests who were dancing around the bride and groom. The bride and groom were very happy. Everyone was clapping and laughing.

When the song ended, the dancers were very thirsty. They asked the servants to refill their wine goblets, but the servants discovered that the stone jugs were empty.

"My friends," said the host, "I am sorry, but I have no more wine to give you."

The guests were very disappointed.

Mary led Jesus by the hand to the host. "Jesus can make more wine," she said. "Please ask the servants to do whatever he requests."

Seeing Mary's faith in her son, the host agreed.

The disciples John and Philip watched Jesus curiously. They loved him, but they did not yet have complete faith in him. "Can Jesus turn water into wine?" asked John.

"I do not know," answered Philip. "Turning water into wine is a miracle. If Jesus can do this, we must follow him wherever he goes."

Mary did not have a doubt. She knew Jesus could do it.

Jesus said to the servants, "Please fill these empty jugs with water."

The servants dashed to the nearby well and pumped water into every available pail, bottle, bowl, and cup. Spilling water as they went, they ran back to Jesus, poured the water into the jugs, and hurried back to the well for more. Finally, each jug was filled to the brim.

One servant eagerly turned to Jesus and asked, "What do you want us to do next?"

Everyone waited for Jesus to reply.

Jesus turned to one of the young servants and said, "Please pour a goblet of water for the wedding host."

The servant girl chose a fine goblet from the table. She carefully filled it and handed it to the host. He took a drink, and all the guests held their breath. "Delicious!" he shouted. "This is the best wine I have ever tasted in my life!"

"Hooray!" shouted the servants and all the guests.

"Praise be to God!" shouted Philip.

"It is a miracle!" said John.

"Bless you, son," said Mary. "I knew you could do it."

Sowing Seeds

Retold by Lisa Harkrader
Illustrated by Flora Jew

Hannah's mother dropped some coins into Hannah's hand.

"Are you sure that you are comfortable going to the market on your own?" asked Hannah's mother.

"Yes, Mama," said Hannah. "I am sure."

"Buy fish at a good price," said Hannah's mother, "but do not take advantage of the fish seller's kindness."

"Yes, Mama," Hannah said.

The market was crowded, but soon everyone was headed toward the sea. They were following a man who was telling stories as he walked.

Hannah loved stories, so she followed the crowd. Everyone stopped at the edge of the sea. The man who was telling stories climbed into a boat so everyone could see him.

Hannah was standing beside an old woman. She tugged on the woman's robe and pointed to the man on the boat.

"Who is he?" Hannah asked.

"His name is Jesus," said the woman, smiling. "His stories open our eyes and show us God's word in a new way."

Jesus looked out over the crowd. His face was filled with kindness. He began speaking.

"A farmer went out to sow his seeds," he said. "As he was scattering the seeds, some fell on the path, and birds ate them."

Hannah nodded. That happened once when she helped her father plant wheat. She had spilled a few seeds, and the birds ate them before she could pick them up.

Hannah listened as Jesus continued.

"Some seeds fell on rocky places, where there was not much soil," he said. "Plants sprang up quickly, because the soil was shallow. But when the sun came up, the plants were scorched, and they withered."

Hannah frowned. Her father told her not to plant seeds in rocky patches because the plants would not get enough water, and they would not have enough soil under them to grow deep roots. Any farmer knew that. When would Jesus get to the good part of the story?

Jesus continued speaking. "Other seeds fell among thorns," he said. "The thorns choked the new plants."

Hannah tugged on the old woman's robe again. "This is not a very good story," she said. "Why does everyone think Jesus is so wise?"

The woman smiled. "Keep listening," she said.

Hannah shook her head, but she kept listening.

"Still other seeds fell on good soil," said Jesus. "Plants sprung up, grew, and yielded a crop a hundred times more than what was planted."

Then Jesus stopped speaking. Hannah waited.

Was the story over? Hannah looked around. The other people in the crowd seemed confused, too. One man asked what the story meant.

"The seed is the word of God," Jesus said. "Those along the path hear it, but the devil comes and takes the word from their hearts and they are not saved. Those on the rock receive the word with joy, but they have no roots. They believe for a while, but when trouble comes upon them, they fall away. Those among thorns hear the word, but then they are choked by life's worries and pleasures, and they do not grow. But the seeds on the good soil hear the word, keep it, and produce a crop."

Hannah smiled. The woman was right. Jesus' story had shown her God's word in a new way.

Hannah ran back toward the market. She found her mother at the fruit stall. "Mama! I understand," she said.

Her mother looked at her. "You understand what, Hannah?" she asked.

"I understand God's word in a new way," Hannah said.

Hannah's mother smiled.

"If I can follow God's word no matter what, I can produce a good crop," Hannah said.

"Jesus was not really talking about plants," Hannah's mother said.

"I know," Hannah said. "He was talking about people. He was talking about me!"

Jesus Walks on Water

Retold by Rebecca Grazulis
Illustrated by Pamela Johnson

Jesus and all his disciples set out at sunrise to share a message of peace. Jesus liked talking to the people, and he was very grateful for his disciples' help. When the sun began to set, Jesus led the disciples to a boat.

"Friends, thank you for teaching with me today," said Jesus. "Please use this boat to go to Capernaum and rest."

The disciples did not want to leave Jesus, but they agreed. It had been a long day, so they got into the boat.

"Will you come with us, Jesus?" asked Peter. "You must be tired also. Let us all go together."

"Do not worry, Peter," replied Jesus. "I will meet you later."

The disciples trusted that Jesus knew what was best. They waved goodbye and pushed the boat away from the shore.

Jesus watched the disciples' boat sail across the Sea of Galilee. He thought about how good his friends were.

"They will help me on my journey," thought Jesus, "and I will show them how much God loves them."

Jesus wanted to find a quiet place where he could talk to God. He decided to climb to the top of a hill, where he kneeled and began to pray.

"Dear Father," he said, "please show me how I can best serve you."

Suddenly, the sky grew dark and stormy, and the wind began to whip through the hills. Jesus thought of his friends traveling on the Sea of Galilee. He searched the horizon and spotted the small boat moving slowly toward Capernaum.

The disciples were safe for now, but the wind began to blow harder, and the storm picked up. Jesus began to worry about his friends. He knew that they would face trouble during a storm.

The disciples were starting to think they might be in danger. The sky had turned black, and they could no longer see into the distance. They rowed and rowed, but Capernaum was still far away.

"We will not be able to reach the shore," Peter said.

The other disciples tried to comfort Peter, but they were also troubled. What would happen if they lost their way? Who could help them?

Soon the wind grew stronger. The waves crashed over the sides of the boat. Now the disciples were wet and tired. It was starting to look like they might never get to Capernaum.

From high on the hill, Jesus saw the boat as it tossed on the waves. He knew the disciples needed his help. He quickly ran down the hill toward the water.

When he reached the shore, Jesus gently placed his foot on top of the water. Soon he was walking on the water toward the boat and his friends.

The disciples saw a man walking toward them on the water. They could not believe their eyes.

"Do not be afraid," Jesus said. "It is your friend Jesus."

Peter was not sure whether it really was Jesus. "Lord, if it is really you," Peter said, "ask me to walk on the water."

"All right," said Jesus. "Come. I will wait for you here."

Peter stepped over the side of the boat. Slowly, he walked on the water toward Jesus. The tall waves crashed around him. He got scared and could not move. He fell into the cold water.

Jesus rescued Peter. The two men climbed into the boat. Peter thanked Jesus.

"Have faith, Peter," Jesus said. "Trust in God."

The Prodigal Son

Retold by Lora Kalkman
Illustrated by Beth Foster Wiggins

Once there was a man who lived on a large estate with his two sons. After working hard all his life, he was finally able to hire servants. Although the man had become quite wealthy, he still worked hard. He insisted that his sons work hard, too. Together, they and their servants tended to the crops and livestock. They worked very hard, and the older son did not mind it.

But the younger son did not like working at all. "Why must we work so hard?" he asked his father. "We are very wealthy. We have servants. We should not have to work."

"Son," his father explained, "our farm has grown large and prosperous because of our hard work. Success comes to those who earn it."

The younger son said that he did not want to work anymore. He asked his father for his share of the family's money. Then to his father's dismay, he went to see the world.

Gleefully, the younger man counted the gold coins in the bag his father had given him. "There are so many!" he thought with delight. "I have can visit the grandest cities, eat the finest foods, and shop in the finest stores."

The young man journeyed to the largest city in the land. When he arrived, he found a very fancy place to live, with silk curtains and velvet furniture. He feasted on the finest foods every night of the week. He wore the most expensive clothes. If he saw something he wanted, he bought it without even a second thought.

"My father and brother are fools," he said to himself. "They are foolish to spend their days working so hard in the fields. They should be enjoying their money like me."

The young man never considered getting a job. After all, he still had plenty of gold in his bag. Even though his father had tried to teach him the value of hard work, the young man never learned the lesson.

One day while the young man was shopping, a bright tunic caught his eye. He opened his bag to pay the shop owner, but it was only then that he realized it was empty. All of his gold was gone!

"How can this be?" he shrieked. "There were so many coins when I came to the city. Did I really spend them all?"

Alas, the young man had spent his entire fortune on things he did not need. Now he had nothing. He did not even have any money to buy a loaf of bread.

The young man walked to a nearby farm and got a job in the fields. He had to work very hard. He did not make very much money, and he often went to bed hungry.

"If I am going to work, I should go home and work for my father," he thought. "Maybe then I will at least have enough to eat."

The young man returned to his father's estate. As he approached the gate, he felt nervous. He knew he had been wrong. Instead of working hard as his father had taught him, he had wasted all of his money on unimportant things. He was so afraid his father would be angry with him that he considered turning away.

Then he saw his father running toward him. To the young man's surprise, his father was smiling. His arms were stretched out for a hug.

"Dear son," his father said. "I am so glad you have come back. I have missed you so much."

The father was so happy his younger son had returned that he threw a big party to celebrate. He gave his son a new robe and shoes. He served all the best foods.

But the older son did not understand. He did not think his father should treat his younger brother so well. After all, his brother had decided to leave and spend all his wealth on unimportant things, while he had stayed and worked hard.

The father noticed his older son's unhappiness. "Why are you upset?" he asked. "Your brother has come home. Are you not happy that your brother is home?"

"Why are you so good to my brother?" the older son asked. "I do not think it is fair."

The father hugged his older son. "Your brother sees his mistakes. We must forgive and love each other, as God loves and forgives us."

The older son considered his father's wise words. Then he turned to his younger brother. "Welcome home," he said.

The Empty Tomb

Retold by Rebecca Grazulis
Illustrated by Peter Fiore

Jesus led his disciples to a garden called Gethsemane. "I am going to pray," said Jesus. "Keep watch over me."

Jesus went a little way from his disciples. He fell to his knees and prayed. He knew that the time of his death was nearing.

Jesus turned to look at the disciples and saw that they were asleep. "Can you not keep watch with me?" asked Jesus.

Then Jesus went to pray for a second time. "Father," he said. "If I must die, let your will be done."

Jesus turned around and found the disciples asleep again. Jesus prayed again. Finally, he woke the disciples.

"The hour has come when I will be given into the hands of sinners," said Jesus. "See! The one who betrays me is here!"

At that moment, Judas, one of the disciples, marched into the garden. He was followed by a crowd of angry people and soldiers who carried spears.

"The man I kiss is Jesus," Judas told the soldiers. "When I kiss him, take him as your prisoner."

Then Judas went and kissed Jesus. The Roman soldiers grabbed Jesus and arrested him. They took him to Pontius Pilate, who was the governor.

"What has this man done wrong?" asked Pilate.

"He must have done wrong, or we would not have arrested him," one of the soldiers said.

"Then judge him," said Pilate. "I cannot."

The crowd and the soldiers knew they needed Pilate's order to put a man to death.

Finally Pilate agreed to question Jesus. "Are you the King of the Jews?" he asked.

"My kingdom is not on this earth," Jesus said. "I was born to the world—to bring the truth."

"I find no guilt with this man," Pilate said to the crowd, "and I need to release someone during the Passover."

"No!" the crowd cried. "Crucify him!"

Pilate tried to release Jesus, but the crowd would not have it. They called out, "If you release Jesus, you are no friend of our ruler Caesar."

Pilate thought the crowd was wrong. "I wash my hands of this," he said. Still, he ordered Jesus to be crucified.

The soldiers wove a crown of sharp thorns and placed it on Jesus' head. "Hail, King of the Jews!" they called as they hit him.

The crowd then made Jesus carry the heavy cross, on which he would be crucified, down the streets of Galilee. Finally they arrived in Golgotha, which means Place of a Skull.

There the soldiers hung Jesus on the cross. Criminals were hanging upon crosses to the right and left of Jesus.

The crowd shouted at Jesus as he hung on the cross. "If you are the Son of God, save yourself!" they cried.

"Father, forgive them," Jesus prayed.

Jesus' mother, Mary, his mother's sister, and Mary Magdalene stood at the foot of the cross. They were very sad. When Jesus saw his mother, he called to her, "Behold your son!"

At noon, darkness covered the entire land. At three o'clock, Jesus called out to his father, "My God, why have you forsaken me?"

After a man gave him a sip of vinegar from a sponge tied to a long stick, Jesus said, "It is finished."

Jesus bowed his head and gave up his spirit. Then the earth began to shake, and rocks split apart.

Soon one of Jesus' disciples, Joseph of Arimathea, asked Pilate if he could take the body of Jesus. Eager to help in any way he could, Pilate agreed.

Joseph wrapped Jesus' body in linen and anointed it with spices. Then he put Jesus' body in a tomb and rolled a large stone in front of the entrance.

Three days later, Mary Magdalene visited the tomb. When she got there she saw that the stone had been rolled away. She ran to Simon Peter and told him.

Simon Peter ran to Jesus' tomb. He stepped inside the tomb and saw that Jesus' body was gone.

Simon Peter left, but Mary Magdalene stood outside the tomb weeping. Soon she crept into the tomb and saw two angels. "Mary," one of the angels said, "why are you crying?"

"Because they have taken away my Lord," she replied tearfully.

Then Mary turned around and saw Jesus. But she did not realize it was him. "Why are you weeping?" asked Jesus. Mary thought Jesus was the gardener, so she said, "Sir, if you have taken the body of Jesus, please tell me where you have put it."

"Mary," Jesus said.

Suddenly Mary knew that it was Jesus.

Mary Magdalene ran to tell the disciples the good news. And soon Jesus appeared to the disciples himself. "Peace be with you," he greeted them.

Then Jesus showed them his hands and his side, so they would believe it was him.

But Thomas, who was not there, did not believe it when he heard that Jesus had arisen. It was eight days before Jesus saw the disciples when they were all together.

"My Lord!" exclaimed Thomas.

"You believe because you have seen me," replied Jesus. "But blessed are they who don't see, but believe. Go and spread the word of God. And remember, I am always with you."

The Promise

Retold by Lora Kalkman
Illustrated by Debbie Pinkney

Jesus rose up, up, up into the sky. The disciples could hardly believe their eyes! Soon all they could see were clouds and brilliant light.

"It is truly amazing," one disciple cried. "He is gone."

"He has simply gone home to his Father," said another.

Then two angels miraculously appeared next to the disciples. The angels were dressed in white. "Why do you stand here looking into the sky?" the angels asked.

The disciples explained what they had seen. They told the angels of the beautiful miracle they had witnessed.

"It *is* a miracle!" the angels agreed.

But Jesus had promised his disciples they would receive a gift. He told the men to wait for the gift in Jerusalem.

In Jerusalem, the disciples went about their daily work. They told as many people as they could about Jesus and his promise to return.

One day, the disciples gathered together to enjoy a meal. It was the day of Pentecost, seven weeks after Jesus had come back to earth after dying on the cross.

As they ate, they heard a loud sound in the sky. They thought it was the wind, but it was not. They were puzzled.

All of a sudden, flames appeared above them. The fire did not burn anything. It seemed to be sending a message, but no one understood what it meant.

Again, the disciples were puzzled. One opened his mouth to speak. To his surprise, he spoke in a foreign language! In fact, all of the disciples could now speak foreign languages.

The disciples soon realized that they had received the gift that Jesus promised. Because they could now speak in many languages, they could tell everyone they met about Jesus.

Before the gift, many people could not understand the disciples. The disciples could not understand them either. Now the disciples could speak to people from every country. They could understand everyone's questions, too.

The gift made the disciples very happy. They were excited to tell everybody about Jesus.

One day, two disciples, Peter and John, were walking through the city. They were going to the temple to pray. Along the way, they stopped to tell people about Jesus.

As they approached the temple gate, they saw a man sitting nearby. He looked sad and hungry. He had a disease and could not walk. He asked Peter and John if they would give him some money to buy a loaf of bread.

"We do not have any money," Peter replied. "But we do have the love of Jesus Christ. Jesus can even make you walk. Stand up and see."

Sure enough, the man rose to his feet and began to walk!

"How did you do that?" a little boy asked Peter.

"We did not make this man walk," Peter replied. "Jesus did. Jesus is the Son of God."

As Peter talked to the crowd, he saw that many little children had gathered around. Peter remembered that Jesus loved little children most of all.

Peter smiled and scooped the boy up into his arms. Then he told all of the little children to gather closer.

"Jesus loves all people, especially little children," Peter said. "Jesus watches over everyone. You can talk to Jesus anytime you want to. Jesus always hears our prayers."

The End